Encounters

Contents

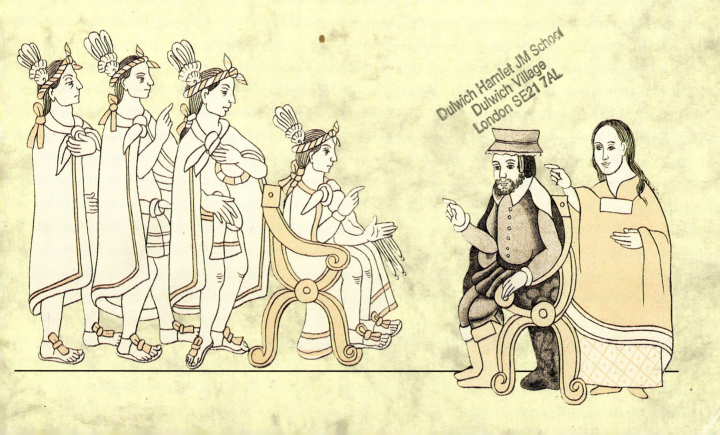

Mexico and the Spaniards

The Land of Mexico

This is Mexico City, the **capital city** of Mexico. Mexico is in Central America.

Five hundred years ago another city stood here. It was the chief city of people called the Aztecs. They ruled over most of the other peoples in the land of Mexico.

Some Mexicans today are related to the Aztecs and speak their language. But most Mexicans speak Spanish because five hundred years ago some Spaniards sailed to Mexico. They fought the Aztecs and took over their **empire**.

Capital city

The chief city of a country.

Empire

A group of countries or peoples ruled over by one country or people.

This is the emblem, or sign, of Mexico. It shows an eagle, sitting on a cactus, eating a snake. It tells an old story about the first Aztecs. In those days they did not have a fixed home. They moved from place to place to find grass for their animals to eat.

Find:
- the eagle
- the cactus
- the snake

The story is that one of their gods told them they would settle down one day and build a city in the middle of a lake. The god said they would find an eagle, sitting on a cactus, eating a snake. This was where they would build their city.

Hundreds of years later they did build a city on an island. They called it Tenochtitlan which, in the Aztec language, means 'City in the middle of the lake'. Today the lake has gone, but Mexico City stands on the same place.

Outside the cities most of Mexico is like this. It is a hot dry land with many mountains.

The First Mexicans

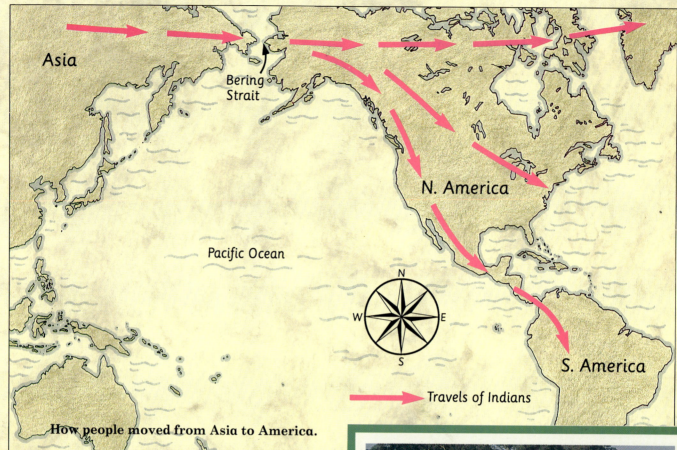

How people moved from Asia to America.

The first Mexicans probably came from Asia. Find Asia on the map. Now find the narrow stretch of sea, called the Bering Strait. It separates Asia and North America.

About ten thousand years ago, in a time called the Ice Age, the sea here froze over in winter. So you could walk across the ice from Asia to North America.

Animals crossed over looking for places where there was grass to eat. People followed because they were hunting the animals. Look on the map to see where they went. They were the first humans to settle in America. Later the ice melted. So they were cut off from Asia.

One of the first peoples to settle in Mexico was called the Maya. They settled there about four thousand years ago. Find where they lived on the map. Some people who live there today are related to the Maya.

This is a Mayan pyramid with a temple on the top. They built their towns and temples in the jungle because they found water there in deep holes in the ground.

The Maya invented their own picture writing.

Here are some of their words carved in stone.

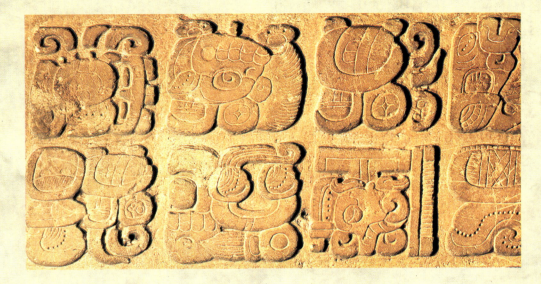

The Maya were also clever artists. This painting on a clay vase shows a Mayan man from an important family drinking from a bowl.

**Find the man's head-dress and clothes.
What does this painting tell you about the way wealthy Mayan men dressed?**

Perhaps he is drinking a chocolate drink invented by the Maya. They called it 'chocolatl'. They made it using beans from the cocoa trees that grew in the forests.
These beans were so valuable they used them as money to buy things in the markets.

Hernan Cortes

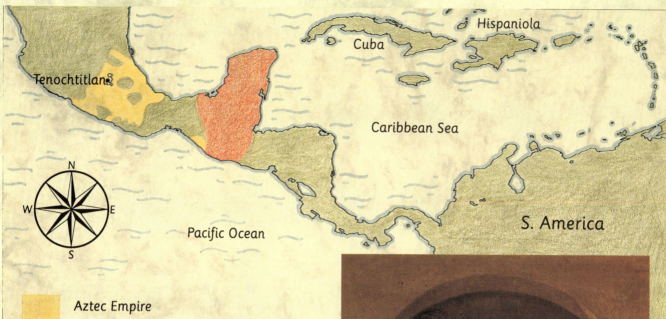

Tenochtitlan

Cuba

Hispaniola

Caribbean Sea

Pacific Ocean

S. America

N
W   E
S

Aztec Empire

Lands of the Maya

In 1492 Christopher Columbus made a voyage across the Atlantic Ocean from Spain to the Caribbean. You can read about it in *Explorations*.

Columbus did not know about America. He thought he had found islands in the East, near Japan which he called Cipangu. He thought they were rich in spices and gold.

The next year, fifteen hundred Spaniards who wanted to make their fortunes left Spain to settle on an island which the Spanish now called **Hispaniola** or New Spain. Find it on the map.

Arawaks lived on the island. The Spaniards tried to make them work in the gold mines. Fighting broke out and about a hundred thousand Arawaks were killed—one in three of those living there. What do you think the remaining Arawaks thought about Europeans?

HERNAN CORTES

This is Hernan Cortes. He left Spain to settle on Hispaniola in 1504, when he was nineteen. By then the Spaniards ruled the whole island and most of the Arawaks were slaves.

The Spaniards wanted to take over other islands. Cortes took part in an attack on Cuba. Find it on the map. He stayed there and became a wealthy landowner.

Hispaniola

We do not know what the Arawaks called this island. Today it is divided into two countries—The Dominican Republic and Haiti.

Governor

The person asked by the King of Spain to rule Cuba.

Cuba is very close to America. Find them both on the map. The Spaniards had heard about the Aztecs and their rich city, Tenochtitlan, in the middle of a lake.

This excited Cortes. He persuaded the Spanish **governor** of Cuba to put him in charge of an army to try to take over the lands of the Aztec Empire.

Christians

People who follow the religion of Christianity. They believe in the life and teachings of Jesus Christ.

Cortes wanted gold and riches. He also wanted the Aztecs to become **Christians.** Most Europeans were Christians at this time. They wanted everyone else in the world to become Christian, even those who believed in other gods.

Cortes took his army to Mexico in eleven ships. Messengers quickly went to tell the Aztec ruler that strange people had landed.

Find:
- the Mexican watching from a tree.
- the Spanish sailor fishing.

This Aztec painting shows Cortes's ships coming towards the shore.

This is part of a picture painted by a Mexican artist about forty years ago. It shows Cortes leading his army into Mexico.

Find:
- Cortes with his sword.
- the large wooden Christian cross.
- the Aztec messenger with gifts. What is he doing?

What is Cortes doing? How is this picture of Cortes different from the one on page 6?

What do you think this artist thought about Cortes?

The Aztecs

The Aztec Empire

Every eighty days the other peoples in the Aztec Empire had to send **tribute** to Tenochtitlan.

The Aztecs used their picture writing to make tribute-sheets like this to show the things the different peoples had to give them.

The Aztecs painted this on paper made from the bark of trees. The Spanish writing was put on later. Some of the things that had to be given to the Aztecs were blankets, animal skins, feathers, cocoa beans, silver, costumes, beads and food. Can you find any of these?

Tribute

Money or goods given by a conquered people to their rulers.

The other Mexican peoples hated the Aztecs. They did not want to pay tribute and they were frightened of the Aztec fighters, or warriors, who were sent to punish them if they did not pay.

Every Aztec boy wanted to be a successful 'warrior', which was the name given to soldiers who were especially brave and successful fighters. It was a way to become rich and famous. To become a warrior you had to capture a lot of prisoners in battle.

The tribute from other peoples made the Aztecs very rich. They built splendid cities.

This is the main square of Tenochtitlan where the **emperor** had his palace.

A Mexican archaeologist drew this picture to show how the square looked in 1519.

Find:

● the pyramids with temples on the top.

● the square building between the pyramids. This was the emperor's palace.

● someone getting out of a canoe. People moved around the city by paddling canoes along canals.

Here are some warriors with their prisoners.

Look at the warriors' clothes. How are they different? How are they the same?
They wore different clothes according to how many prisoners they had captured.
Warriors were the only people allowed to wear bright clothes and jewellery.

Emperor	Canal
Chief ruler of an empire.	A water channel specially built for boats to travel along.

The Aztec Way of Life

There was no room to grow all the food that people needed in Tenochtitlan so the Aztecs built islands in the lake using leaves and sticks. They covered them with mud and planted gardens on them. Some of them are still there today. They are known as the 'floating gardens of Mexico'.

These tourists are visiting the floating gardens just outside Mexico City. They have changed very little since Aztec times.

Here is a farmer planting corn seeds to grow **maize** which was the Aztecs' most important food.

Find:

- where the farmer keeps the seeds he is going to plant.
- what the farmer uses to make the holes for the seeds.

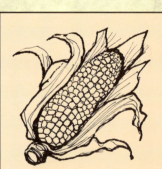

Maize

A type of corn which grew only in America until the Spaniards took it from Mexico to Europe five hundred years ago.

Today there are many different sorts of maize. We call one of them 'sweet corn'.

Slaves

People who had to work for other people without having any wages. They could be sold by their owners to someone else.

Here are two farmworkers storing the maize for the winter. They used it to make porridge and 'tortillas' which are thin pancakes made from maize flour.

Farmers also had to help do other work such as building temples and roads and fighting in wars, if they were told to. If they did well and took prisoners, they could become warriors.

Farming was hard work but farmers were free. They could even own **slaves.**

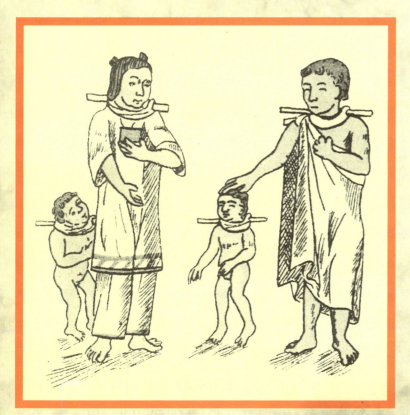

Some slaves came from other peoples and were prisoners of war. Some were Aztecs who sold themselves because they wanted to be looked after in someone else's house in return for working for them. Aztec owners looked after their slaves well.

These slaves are wearing wooden bars across the backs of their necks to show that they are not free.

This is part of a market. Every Aztec town had a market where people went to exchange goods.

Find:

- the things for sale laid out on the ground.
- the man and the woman sitting down. Are there any clues about who owns the stall and who is the customer?

The Aztecs used cocoa beans instead of money. They were easy to carry and everyone wanted them because they liked to make 'chocolatl'.

Here is a doctor rubbing her patient's back with the leaves of a plant. The Aztecs knew that some plants can help to cure pain or illness.

Here is a baby being given its name.

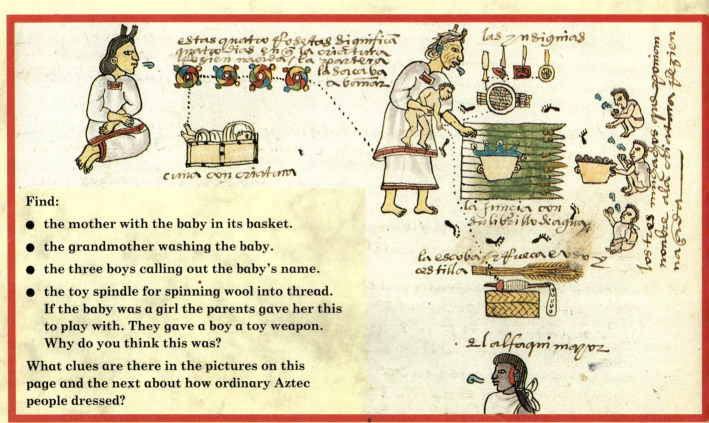

Find:

- the mother with the baby in its basket.
- the grandmother washing the baby.
- the three boys calling out the baby's name.
- the toy spindle for spinning wool into thread. If the baby was a girl the parents gave her this to play with. They gave a boy a toy weapon. Why do you think this was?

What clues are there in the pictures on this page and the next about how ordinary Aztec people dressed?

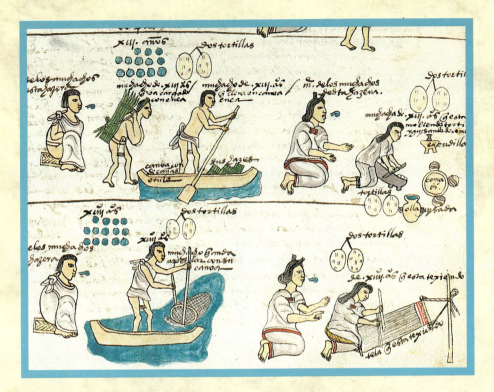

Here is a father teaching his son to carry firewood and to paddle a canoe.

Find the small blue circles. They add up to how many years old the boy is.

Here is a mother teaching her daughter to grind corn and to use a loom to weave cloth.

Find the big white circles. They show how many tortillas the child should be given to eat each day.

Most children were taught by their parents until they were about sixteen. Then they went to school to learn about the history of the Aztec people and how to worship the gods.

Here is a wedding. Parents decided whom a child was to marry. They were helped by older women called 'matchmakers'.

Find:

- the matchmaker carrying the girl into the house of the boy's parents.
- the people carrying flaming torches.
- the bride and bridegroom. At the end of the ceremony their clothes were tied together to show they were married.
- the old men and women sitting at the side. They made long speeches at the wedding.

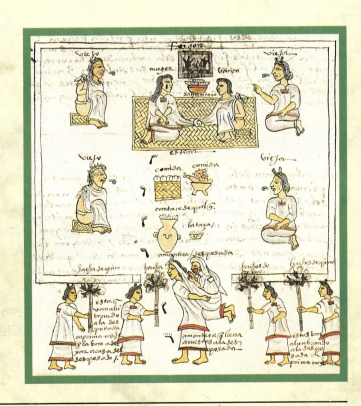

Gods and Religious Life

The Aztecs worshipped many different gods.

This is a statue of Coatlicue, the mother of all the Aztec gods.

This stone, called the 'Calendar Stone', stood in the middle of the main square in Tenochtitlan.

Find the circle that goes round the four squares in the middle. The twenty pictures in it are the signs for the Aztec days. They had three hundred and sixty five days in a year, divided into eighteen months of twenty days each. That left five days that did not belong to a month. These were unlucky days.

Find the face in the centre of this stone. It is the face of the sun. The Aztecs believed that the sun was very important because it brought them light and heat each day. They had three main gods; the god of war, the god of wind, and the chief of them, who was the god of sun.

The Aztecs believed they had to keep their gods happy and strong by giving them the best possible food. In return the gods would look after them. They thought human hearts were the best food for the gods because a person's heart is the most valuable thing they have.

Here are Aztec priests cutting people's hearts out to offer to the gods. They usually offered the hearts of prisoners of war. That is why Aztec warriors had to capture prisoners alive.

Find:
- the two priests. What is each one doing?
- the two prisoners of war.
- the people watching. What do you think they are feeling?

The priests used knives like this to cut out hearts.

Find the figure on the handle of the knife. It shows a warrior called an 'Eagle Knight' who served the chief god. You had to be a very skilful and brave fighter to become an Eagle Knight.

This is the only important Aztec god who did not expect to be offered human hearts. He is Quetzalcoatl, god of the wind. He was also god of life because he blew life into things.

Quetzalcoatl means 'feathered snake'. Find the snake.

The Aztecs held a big celebration for the gods every month. There were processions and dances as well as **sacrifices**.

They played some of their games in honour of the gods too.

This is a court for playing a team game with a ball. You had to get the ball through the ring on the wall but you weren't allowed to hit it with your hands. You could use only your elbows, hips or legs.

The ball court at the Mayan city of Chichen Itza. Aztec courts were like this. They were usually near temples. The ball for the game was made of hard rubber. Europeans saw rubber for the first time when the Spaniards saw the Aztecs playing this game.

Sacrifices

An offering to a god is called a sacrifice. The Aztecs sacrificed human hearts.

Here is a ballplayer in action.

This is a Mayan sculpture. Find the clothing the player uses to protect himself. What clues does this give you about the game?

Art, Crafts and Technology

This is a feather head-dress. It was part of the costume worn by priests on special occasions when they were playing the part of a god.

Aztec craftspeople were very clever at making costumes and head-dresses out of feathers.

They made all sorts of patterns by tying the stems of feathers into costumes when they were being woven.

Here is a feather worker.

Here is a gold worker making a large ornament.

The gold worker is using a curved knife. The blade was made from a sharp stone. The Aztecs did not use any tools made of iron though woodworkers did use some made of copper.

Aztec gold workers were very skilful. Here is a gold buckle showing the face of a god.

The goldworker has made this buckle in the shape of a mask.

Find the patterns on the face.

The Aztecs liked to make mosaics. Mosaics are pictures or patterns made by sticking together small pieces of coloured material, usually stone.

Here is a mosaic mask. It was made out of a human skull with the back cut away.

**Find the two sorts of stones used by the artist.
The greeny-blue ones are called 'turquoise'.
The black ones are called 'lignite'.**

The Aztecs used clay to make pottery bowls, cups, plates and vases. This is an Aztec bowl.

They made their pots using strips of clay. They worked the strips together with their fingers to make the shape they wanted.

Here is an Aztec painting of a pattern of snakes. Snakes were important to the Aztecs because they were the sign for life.

Aztec artists made carvings using stone tools. They did not have metal ones.

This is a feathered serpent on the side of a temple to the god Quetzalcoatl.

This is an Eagle Knight, a warrior specially chosen to serve the chief god.

Find the knight's head-dress. What is it? What clues does this carving give you about how the Aztecs thought about the Eagle Knights?

Buildings

The Aztecs built enormous buildings like this pyramid using very simple tools. First they made a big pile of earth and stones. Then they built the walls and steps around it.

They used sharp flintstones to chip big blocks of stone into the right shape. They used sand and water to polish them.

This model shows how a finished pyramid, with its temple on top, probably looked.

Hernan Cortes and the Conquest of the Aztecs

When Hernan Cortes sailed with his army from Cuba to
Mexico in 1519, the Aztec emperor, Montezuma, had
been ruler for sixteen years. He was very rich and powerful.
He was a brave fighter and he commanded thousands of soldiers.

Cortes had an army of only five hundred men.
Yet when Montezuma heard Cortes had landed he did not
send his army to fight him. Instead, he sent presents to Cortes.

This is one of the presents he sent.

Montezuma did not fight Cortes because he thought he might be the god Quetzalcoatl. The Aztecs believed Quetzalcoatl had once been a Mexican ruler and that he was going to come back to rule again.

They worked out the day Quetzalcoatl was going to come back. It was the same day that Cortes landed. They also believed Quetzalcoatl had a white face and black beard and wore a feathered head-dress.

Here is an Aztec picture of Cortes. Messengers told Montezuma that Cortes had a white face and black beard and wore a feather in his helmet. No wonder Montezuma thought he might be the god.

Find:
- Cortes
- the Aztec messenger
- the woman talking with Cortes. She is a Mexican who learnt Spanish and became Cortes's interpreter and adviser. The Spaniards called her Dona Marina.

Interpreter

Someone who helps two people who speak different languages to understand what they are saying to each other.

Montezuma said the god could take over the Empire once he was dead. He sent presents to Cortes and asked him to go away till then.

Cortes wanted to go to Tenochtitlan. He ordered all his ships to be burnt. Then, even though he thought the Mexicans would attack his army, he started the long march through deserts and over mountains to the Aztec capital.

Some Mexicans joined him. Here they are helping the Spaniards in a battle.

Find:
- the Spaniards
- their Mexican allies
- the other Mexicans they are fighting

The Mexicans did not have horses. How do you think horses helped the Spaniards?

Cortes did not know how important it was that Montezuma thought he was a god. But he did know he could not defeat the Aztecs if Montezuma ordered his army to fight.

He decided to pretend he had come to Mexico to trade peacefully. That way he hoped to be allowed to go into Tenochtitlan. Then he thought he might find ways to take over the city and tell the Aztecs about Christianity.

The Spaniards marched over one of the three narrow **causeways** that went over the lake to the city. Then Montezuma came out of the city to meet Cortes.

Both these pictures show the meeting between Montezuma and Cortes. One is by an Aztec artist and the other by a Spanish artist.

In each picture find:

● **Montezuma**

● **Cortes**

● **Dona Marina**

● **the presents offered by Montezuma to Cortes.**

How accurately do you think the Spanish artist has shown the Aztecs?

Which picture do you think gives the best impression of what this meeting was really like?

Causeways

A causeway is a raised road that crosses over water.

Montezuma welcomed Cortes to the city and invited the Spaniards to stay in a palace in the main square. It probably looked like this.

This is an Aztec drawing of Montezuma's palace.

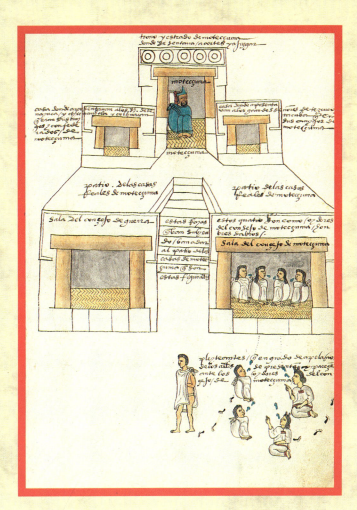

Montezuma still thought Cortes was a god. He hoped he would go away once he saw how well the Emperor ruled.

Next Cortes asked Montezuma to go to live with the Spaniards in their palace. This gave Cortes even more power over Montezuma. Now he could tell Montezuma what orders to give the Aztecs. Cortes was the real ruler of the Empire.

Then the governor of Cuba sent an army to check up on what Cortes was doing. So Cortes left a man called Alvarado in charge of eighty men and marched off with the rest.

They defeated the governor's army and most of the soldiers joined Cortes. Now he had fifteen hundred men.

This picture tells what happened while Cortes was away. Alvarado heard the Aztecs were going to attack his men. Instead of finding out if this was true he decided to attack first while people were dancing after a sacrifice.

Montezuma only just managed to stop the Aztecs from killing the Spaniards in revenge.

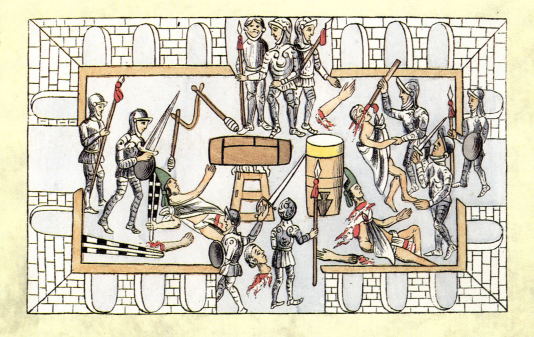

The chief Aztecs decided Montezuma was ruling badly. So they chose a new emperor. Cortes did not know this. He marched his army back into Tenochtitlan. Then the Aztecs surrounded the palace.

Here are the Spaniards and their Mexican allies trapped inside. Cortes made Montezuma stand on the wall to tell the Aztecs not to fight. But they threw stones at him and hit him on the head. Three days later he died.

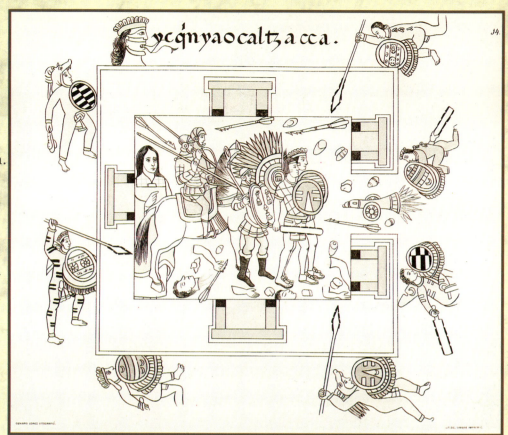

Find the Spanish gun. The Aztecs had never seen guns before.

The Spaniards decided to try to escape over a causeway at night. The Aztecs found out and attacked them from canoes. They killed a thousand Spaniards, but five hundred got away including Cortes and Dona Marina.

Now Cortes planned to capture Tenochtitlan. He had this map of the city made for him. It was a very difficult city to attack because it was surrounded by water.

Find:
- the main square.
- the causeways.
- the towns round the edge of the lake.

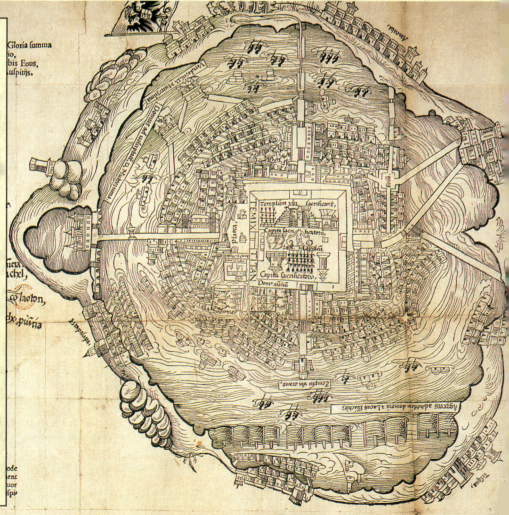

Aqueduct

A channel of pipeline for carrying water.

It took the Spaniards two months to capture Tenochtitlan.

The pictures show how they managed to do it.

Find:

- **Spanish boats**
- **Spanish guns**
- **Aztec boats**
- **Aztec soldiers.**

Which side do you think had the strongest weapons?

First they built boats and put guns in them. They sunk the Aztecs' boats and then fired at the city. They also broke the **aqueduct** that carried water from the mainland to the people in the city.

Then they fought their way along the causeways. They were helped by Mexicans who did not like the Aztecs.

Find:

- the causeway.
- Aztecs defending it.
- Mexicans and Spaniards attacking along the causeway and from boats. How do you think the boats helped?

Here is the Aztec emperor surrendering to Cortes. Cortes ordered Tenochtitlan to be destroyed and he said Mexico now belonged to the king of Spain.

What Happened after the Spanish Conquest?

The Aztec People

This Aztec picture tells what happened
after the conquest.
The Spaniards took over most of the
land and made the Aztecs work for
them as slaves.

chalchicueyca

These Aztecs are building a Spanish fort.
What are they being made to carry?

Find:

● the cross. The Spaniards wanted the
Aztecs to become Christians.

● the Spaniard beating an Aztec. Spanish
masters did not look after slaves as well
as Aztec masters used to do.

The Spaniards wanted the Aztecs to stop sacrificing humans to the gods. They tried to teach them about Christianity.

They pulled down their temples and built Christian churches instead.

Many of those churches still stand in Mexico today. This is one of them. Christian priests started schools where Mexicans learnt Spanish.

The Spaniards also taught the Aztecs to use the wheel which they did not know about before. And they gave them iron tools to use instead of stone ones.

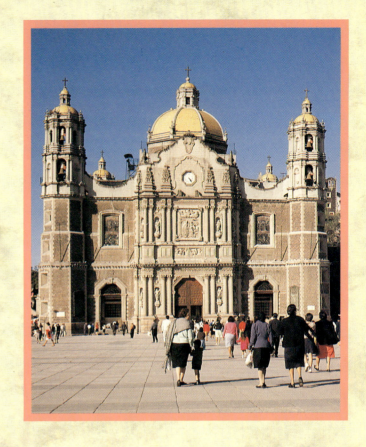

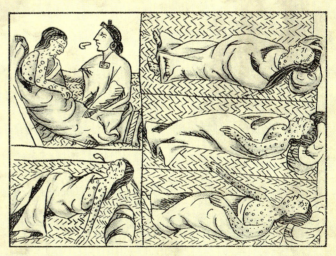

This Aztec drawing tells of the diseases the Spaniards took to Mexico. Illnesses such as colds, measles and smallpox did not exist in Mexico until the Spaniards arrived. Thousands of Aztecs died of them.

The Spaniards ruled Mexico for three
hundred years. Then they agreed to let
the Mexicans rule themselves.

A Mexican artist, called Diego Rivera, painted this picture about
forty years ago. It shows his ideas about Cortes's conquest of Mexico
and the way the Spaniards treated the Aztecs afterwards.

Lands ruled by
the Spaniards

N. America

Mexico
Mexico City

Find:

- **Cortes. He is shown once at the front
  being given money and once in the top
  left holding a sword.**

- **the Spaniards. What are they doing?**

- **the Aztecs. What are they doing?**

**What do you think Hernan Cortes would
say about this picture if he could see it?
What do you think Montezuma would say?**

The Spanish Empire and Trade

About twenty years after Cortes conquered Mexico, another Spaniard leading a small army, Francisco Pizarro, defeated the Incas of Peru in South America. Then he ruled their lands in the name of the king of Spain.

Now the Spaniards had an empire in America. Find the lands they ruled on the map.

Europeans started to call America the 'New World' because it was new to them. The Spaniards who went to settle in the New World wanted to start a new life but they also wanted the things they were used to in the Old World.

Spanish ships sailed to Mexico and Peru loaded with things the settlers wanted that were unknown in America.

Atlantic Ocean

horses, cows, pigs and chickens

wheat

They took to the New World

apples, oranges, lemons, peaches and cherries

almonds, walnuts and chestnuts

roses and lilies

Caribbean Sea

Central America

They took back to Spain

chocolate and coffee

mahogany

tomatoes and avocados

S. America

turkeys

guavas

rubber

maize

Pacific Ocean

On the return journey the ships carried the gold, silver and slaves that the Spaniards at home most wanted from their empire. They also took back things that were new to Europeans and which they soon learned to like.

Remembering The Past

The story of the Spaniards and Mexico started with the voyage of Christopher Columbus. If Columbus had not tried to reach the East by sailing across the Atlantic Ocean, the Spaniards might never have gone to live in the Caribbean and Cortes might never have taken over the empire of the Aztecs.

This statue of Columbus stands in Barcelona. It was put up so that people will remember the famous voyage he made in 1492.

Today people argue about whether or not we should remember Columbus's voyage with pride. Some say we should because he was a brave sailor and because the Spaniards and then other Europeans found America and went to live there.

Some say we should be ashamed because the Spaniards destroyed the way of life of the people who lived in America already, such as the Arawaks in the Caribbean and the Aztecs in Mexico.

What do you think?